This book is due for return by the last date shown above.
To avoid paying fines please renew or return promptly.

Portsmouth
CITY COUNCIL
LEISURE SERVICE

CL-1

Series consultant: Dr Dorothy Rowe

The author and publisher would like to thank the staff
and pupils of the following schools for their help in the
making of this book: St Barnabas Church of England
Primary School, Pimlico; Mayfield Primary school,
Cambridge; St Peter's Church of England Primary
School, Sible Hedingham.

A CIP catalogue record for this book
is available from the British Library.

ISBN 0-7136-6085-6

Reprinted 2003
First paperback edition published 2001
First published in hardback in 1997 by
A & C Black Publishers Ltd
37 Soho Square, London W1D 3QZ
www.acblack.com

Text copyright © 1997 Althea Braithwaite
Photographs copyright © 1997 Charlie Best
Illustrations copyright © 1997 Conny Jude

A & C Black uses paper produced with elemental
chlorine-free pulp, harvested from managed sustainable forests.

Printed in Hong Kong through Colorcraft Ltd.

Feeling Angry

Althea

Photographs by
Charlie Best

Illustrations by
Conny Jude

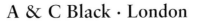

A & C Black · London

What does it mean to be 'angry'?

Sometimes you may feel a bit cross or grumpy. It might be because you aren't feeling very well, or because you have to do something you don't like.

Do I have to come to Aunty Jane's, Dad?

Mum's cross with me because my room's a mess!

People can be grumpy without losing their temper and getting really angry.

Being angry means more than feeling cross or annoyed.
The anger builds up inside and seems to fill your head.

It's as though I'm full of hot steam and all hyped up inside.

My face feels as though it's burning.

My voice goes hard and my skin feels tight.

I feel as though my stomach is all knotted up.

How do you feel when you're angry?

5

We sometimes get angry when we really want something to turn out well, and it doesn't.

Richard says, "I get wound up when I'm trying to make a model and it keeps falling apart."

What other things make us angry?

When I know I'm in the wrong, or feel guilty about something

When my older brother makes me feel small in front of my friends

If I trip over a step, I get angry with the step!

Everyone gets angry at times.

Sometimes you may need to get angry. If someone has broken one of your toys, or treated you unfairly, you have every right to be angry with them.

I get very angry when the others all pick on me.

What makes you angry?

Sometimes it's easy to see when people are angry. You can tell by just looking at them. They may turn pale, or go red in the face.

Do you know how you look when you are really angry?

My friend clenches her fists, like this.

How do you act when you're angry?

Some people go very quiet, and won't say anything. Other people have to let their feelings out.

It makes me want to scream to get it out of my system.

I say lots of things I don't mean.

Jacob says, "When I lose my temper, I lose control and hit out in all directions. I find it very scary - and so does everyone else."

9

Exploding with anger can cause problems - you can't always let yourself do it.
Can you think of any ways to let your anger out, without hurting yourself or other people?

Sometimes it helps to get away on your own. Natalie says, "I stamp all the way up the stairs, and slam my bedroom door. Everyone knows when I'm angry! Then I lie down on my bed and fall asleep - being angry makes me very tired!"

11

We all need time to calm down after we've been angry. Richard says, "Before I can say I'm sorry, I have to do something to make myself feel better. I play computer games or read one of my books."

13

We all have to learn to deal with our anger. It sometimes helps to talk about it.

When we are out, Mum and Dad are so busy enjoying the walk, they won't listen to me.

If you tell another person what is making you angry, they may be able to help or suggest a solution.
If you are still too angry to talk about it, try to wait until you have calmed down.

Holly remembers: "I was very angry with Grandad for dying. He didn't say goodbye to me, and I wanted to tell him that I loved him.

I told my friend Jasmine about it. When I was talking, I started to remember some of the fun things we did together. Just talking about it made me feel less angry and less sad. After a while, remembering the good times we had together became the most important thing."

It usually helps to talk to someone that you're angry with. If you can admit you are angry and explain why, it should help them to understand. It will make you feel better too.

Of course, if you are both very angry, it may be impossible to talk.

It's best to wait until you've calmed down before you say anything. Try not to shout or use angry words. If the other person is still very angry, they may not listen properly - you may have to start again.

Promise you'll listen to me, then I'll listen to you.

They may have good reasons for being angry too. If you are both too angry to talk calmly, it's better to say 'let's talk about it later'.

How do others react when you get angry?

Some adults don't know how to cope with other people's anger, and they get frightened. Then they get angry too.

I get into deep trouble when I'm angry. They never ask why I'm upset.

It always ends up with me being sent to my room!

Adults may not take time to find out what has made you so angry. Instead you may get punished for being badly behaved.
If you get sent to your room, at least it will give you time to calm down and stop feeling angry.

When people are angry with you, do you always know the reason? It can be confusing when you don't know why someone is angry.

It may be because of something you have done. If so, perhaps you can find out, say sorry and make it up.

I used to make everyone cross without knowing it! Now I have stopped trying to chatter to them when they are working.

When someone gets angry with you, it may be because someone else has made them angry. Or they may be tired or upset about something else.

Sometimes, when Mum's really tired, she loses her temper and shouts at me. It's usually over nothing. Later she says sorry.

Try to find out why they are angry. When someone gets angry with you, it doesn't mean that the person doesn't like you, even though it may feel like that at the time.

It's important to try to forget the nasty things people say to hurt you when they are angry. Afterwards they usually wish they hadn't said them.

How do you make up, after you have been very angry with a friend or with a member of your family? It can be difficult to say sorry. It may be easier to do something nice for them.

Sian says, "When I've been angry with my friend, we give each other a big hug, or give each other a little present."

We just say 'Friends?', then it's alright.

You might even find that you can laugh about it afterwards. The important thing is to make friends again, and show that you care and are sorry. We have to be prepared to forgive other people and forget about our arguments. We should forgive ourselves too, for getting angry to start with.

For teachers and parents

A note from Dorothy Rowe

Parents and teachers know that feeling angry is a common problem for children. But they sometimes forget that in order to help, they must first find out how the child sees the problem. A child won't see the situation in the same way as an adult, because no two people ever see things in exactly the same way.

Remembering this, an adult will not assume that they know what is wrong with a child, but will explore alternative reasons for the child's anger. They might ask themselves, 'Does this boy deal with anger in the way he sees his father dealing with his own anger?', or, 'Does this boy get angry when he's frightened?'. It's possible to think up dozens of alternative answers to the question, 'Why does this child behave in this way?'. Doing so helps the adult to ask better questions. However, the answer can only come from the child.

Feeling angry isn't a problem we can solve once and for all, but a dilemma we face all our lives. To help a child understand this, the adult should not pretend to have solved the problem, but rather be prepared to talk about their own difficulties in dealing with it. This way, the adult and the child can explore the dilemma together.

Everyone gets angry at times, and sometimes with good reason. But people have to learn how to control their anger; even when it's justified, they still need to find ways to channel their anger.

To start a discussion, and to get everyone involved, both you and the children could write a list of all the things that make you angry, then compare your lists. If you think that your lists would be too long, you could start off by compiling a list of specific situations which often make people angry. Then, with the children, rate each in terms of whether they make you feel 'very angry', or only 'annoyed', or whether you 'don't mind' them at all. Examples might include:

- Tripping over a step or making a fool of yourself in some way.

- Being wrongly accused of eating the last biscuit, or taking something without permission.

- Someone borrowing something which belongs to you, without asking.

Many of the reasons for anger and the ways of coping with it can be discussed page by page when going through the book again. However, the following may prove useful starting points:

Page 4
There are sure to be many other descriptions of how people feel when they are angry.

Page 6
It's often particularly important to us that things turn out the way we want them to. When they don't, it can sometimes make us very angry.

Some people hate making a fool of themselves, and get very angry when they do; others clown their way through mishaps, and don't seem to mind them. It might be possible to learn to laugh at yourself when you are teased, or someone makes a joke about you, instead of getting angry.

Page 9
Some people become so agitated when they are angry that they don't know what to do with themselves.

Page 10
Small children are often prone to temper tantrums. We all like life to be organised and under control, and it can be very frightening when everything seems to fall apart. The most important thing is for the individual to find ways of coping with these moments.

Page 11
Other suggestions may be to write a description or paint a picture of how you feel when you are angry. Sometimes, something as simple as punching a cushion may help to get rid of anger in a safe way.

Page 12
Children often find that they can make themselves feel better by talking about how they feel to a pet, or to one of their toys.

Often, just thinking about things that you care about or enjoy doing, can help to calm you down.

Page 15
This is a whole area of anger that some people don't recognise. People often feel angry when someone they care about dies. However, many feel that they shouldn't show anger, and so may attempt to repress it.

Page 16
Try suggesting that children count to 10 or 100, and even back again, before trying to talk.

Page 21
It may be better for the child to keep quiet at the time, and wait until later to ask why the other person was angry.

Further reading

Children may find it interesting and helpful to have a look at some of the following story books which also deal with the subject of feeling angry.

Hiawyn Oram
Angry Arthur
Andersen Press (1993)

Jenny Wagner
John Brown, Rose and the Midnight Cat
Viking (1991)

Diana Wyn Jones
The Ogre Downstairs
Macmillan (1996)